CHART H... OF 2018-2019

ISBN 978-1-5400-4759-5

HAL•LEONARD®

Visit Hal Leonard Online at
www.halleonard.com

Contact us:
Hal Leonard
7777 West Bluemound Road
Milwaukee, WI 53213
Email: info@halleonard.com

In Europe, contact:
Hal Leonard Europe Limited
42 Wigmore Street
Marylebone, London, W1U 2RN
Email: info@halleonardeurope.com

In Australia, contact:
Hal Leonard Australia Pty. Ltd.
4 Lentara Court
Cheltenham, Victoria, 3192 Australia
Email: info@halleonard.com.au

BETTER NOW

Words and Music by AUSTIN POST,
CARL ROSEN, ADAM FEENEY, LOUIS BELL,
WILLIAM WALSH and KAAN GUNESBERK

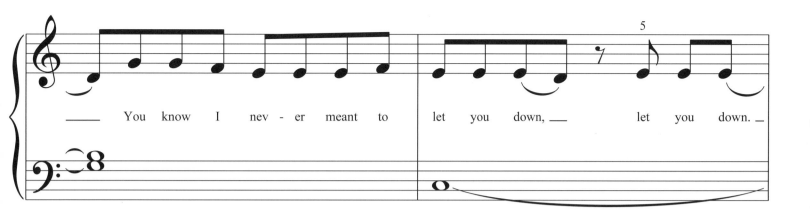

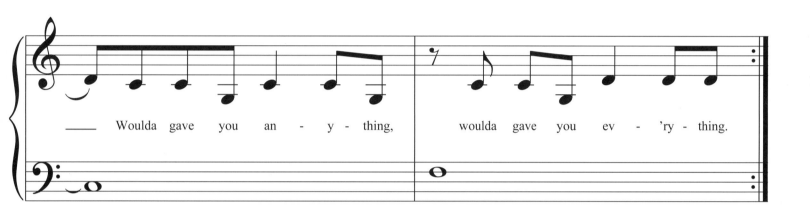

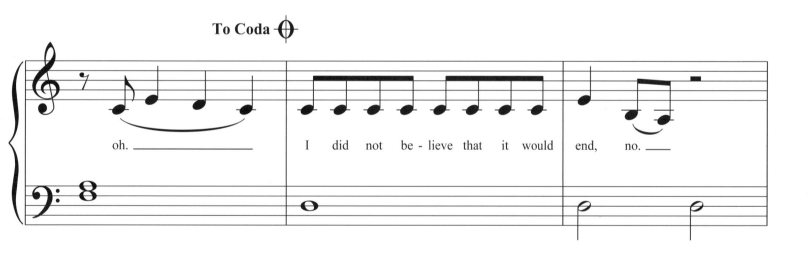

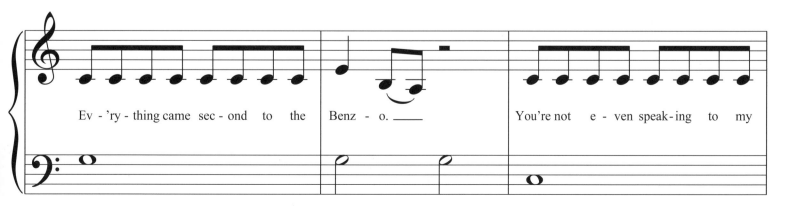

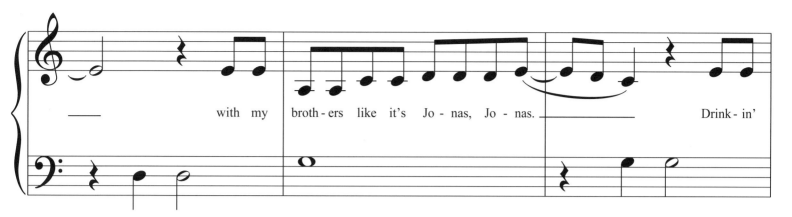

with my broth - ers like it's Jo - nas, Jo - nas. _____ Drink - in'

D.S. al Coda
(with repeat)

Hen - ny and I'm try - na for - get, _____ but I can't get this out - ta my head.

CODA

I seen you with your oth - er dude. He seemed like he was pret - ty

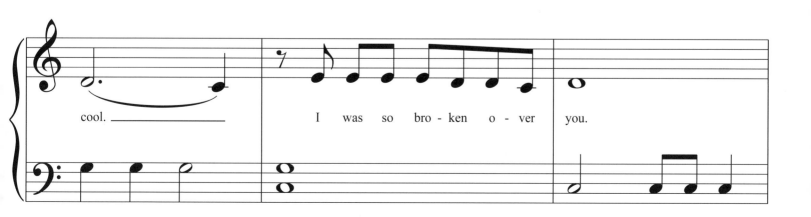

cool. _____ I was so bro - ken o - ver you.

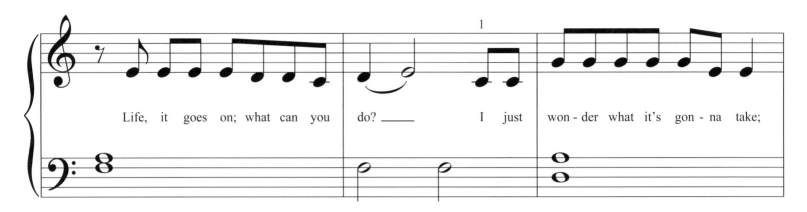

Life, it goes on; what can you do? _____ I just won-der what it's gon-na take;

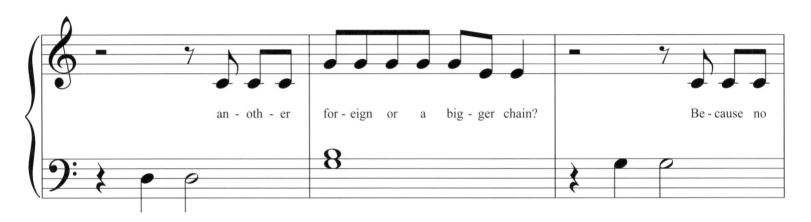

an - oth - er for - eign or a big - ger chain? Be - cause no

mat - ter how my life has changed, I keep on look - ing back on bet - ter days.

You prob-'ly think that you are bet - ter now, _ bet - ter now. _____ You on - ly say that 'cause I'm

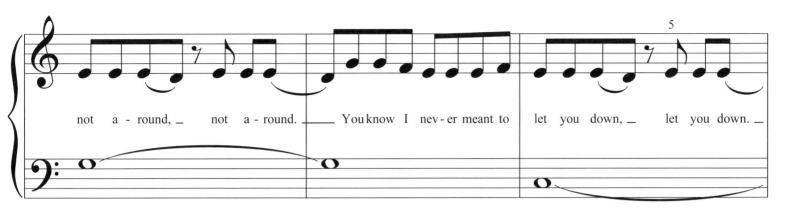

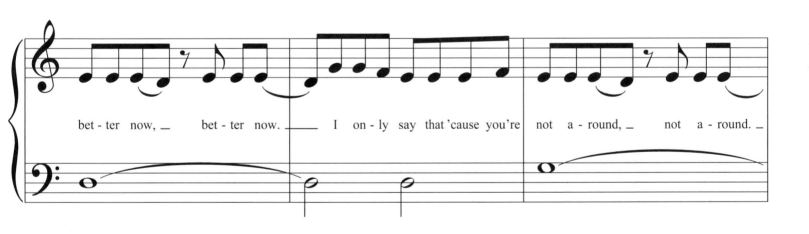

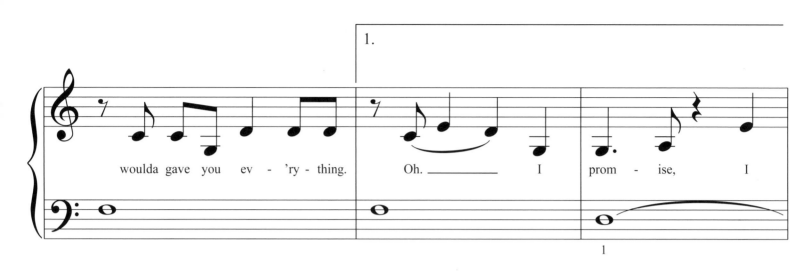

woulda gave you ev - 'ry - thing. Oh. _____ I prom - ise, I

1

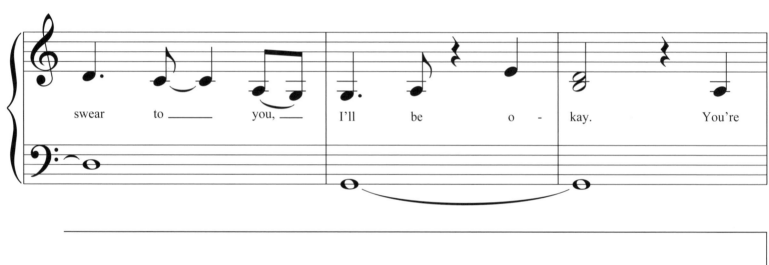

swear to _____ you, _____ I'll be o - kay. You're

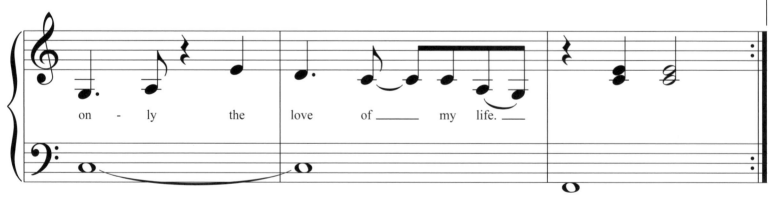

on - ly the love of _____ my life. _____

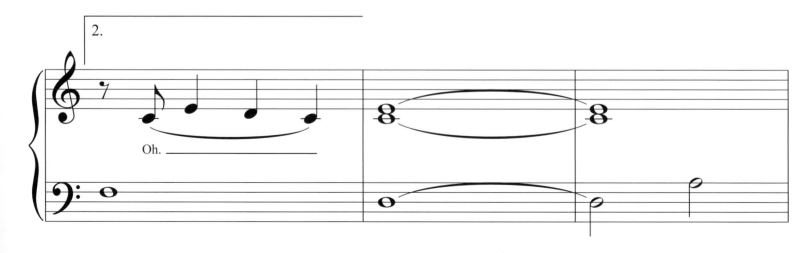

Oh. _____

BREATHIN

Words and Music by ARIANA GRANDE,
SAVAN KOTECHA, MAX MARTIN and IIYA

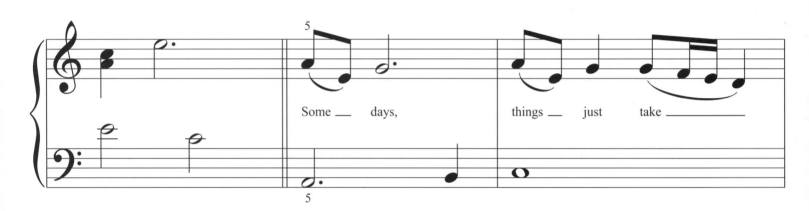

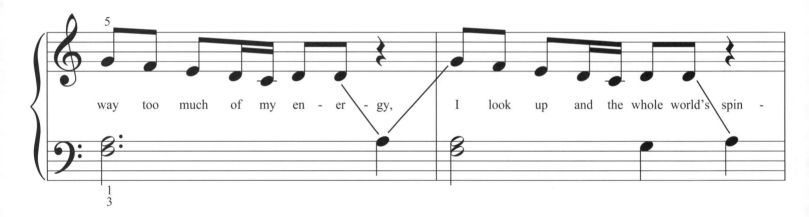

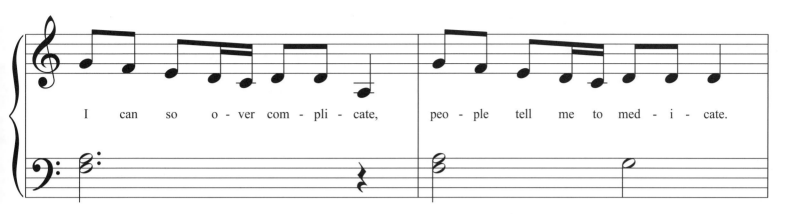

I can so o - ver com - pli - cate, peo - ple tell me to med - i - cate.

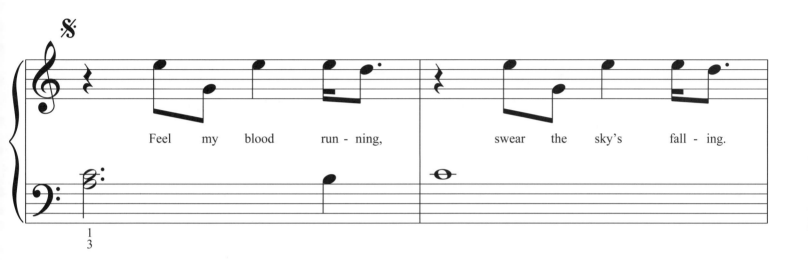

Feel my blood run - ning, swear the sky's fall - ing.

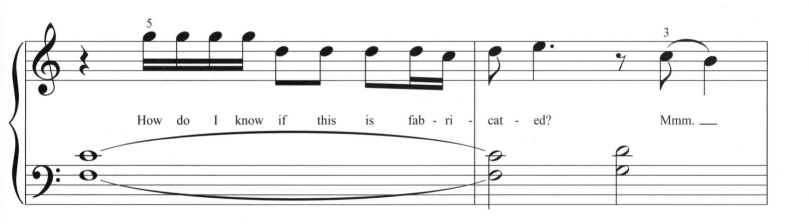

How do I know if this is fab - ri - cat - ed? Mmm. ___

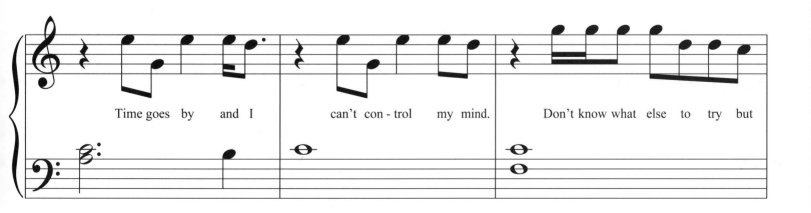

Time goes by and I can't con - trol my mind. Don't know what else to try but

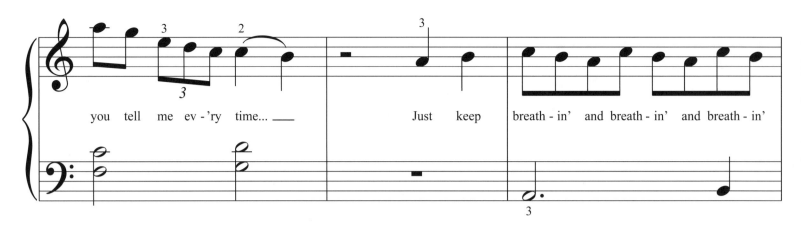

you tell me ev-'ry time... ____   Just keep   breath - in' and breath - in' and breath - in'

and breath-in'.   I   know I've got to keep,   keep on   breath-in'.   Just keep

breath - in'   and   breath - in'   and   breath - in'   and   breath - in'. _____   I

To Coda ⊕

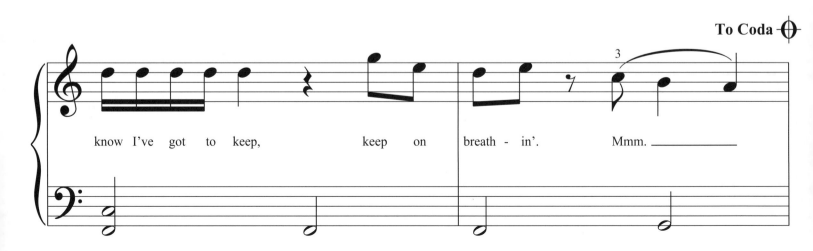

know I've got to keep,   keep   on   breath - in'.   Mmm. _____

D.S. al Coda

CODA

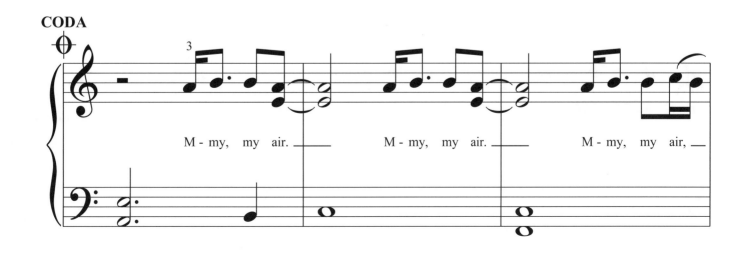

_____ my air. _____ M - my, my air. _____ M - my, my air. __

_____ M - my, my air, yeah. _____ Just keep

breath - in' and breath - in' and breath - in' and breath - in'. Oh, I

know I've got to keep, keep on breath - in'. Just keep breath-in' and breath-in' and breath-in'

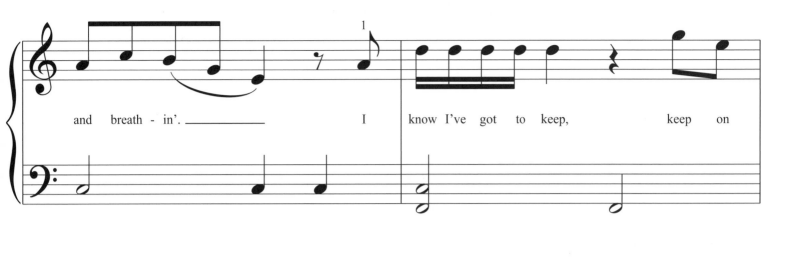

HIGH HOPES

Words and Music by BRENDON URIE, SAMUEL HOLLANDER,
WILLIAM LOBBAN BEAN, JONAS JEBERG, JACOB SINCLAIR,
JENNY OWEN YOUNGS, ILSEY JUBER, LAUREN PRITCHARD
and TAYLOR PARKS

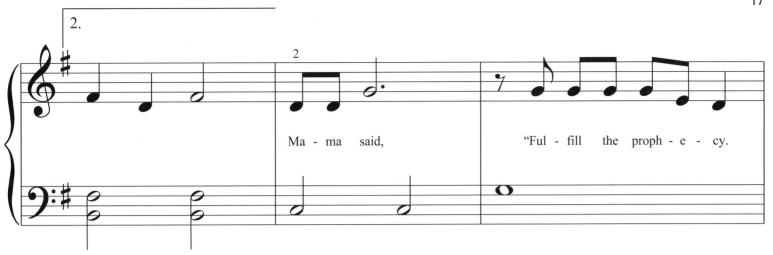

Ma - ma said, "Ful - fill the proph - e - cy.

Be some-thing great. ___ Go make a leg - a - cy." Man - i - fest des - ti - ny.

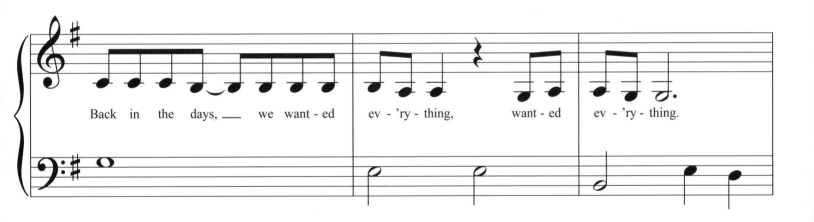

Back in the days, ___ we want - ed ev - 'ry-thing, want - ed ev - 'ry - thing.

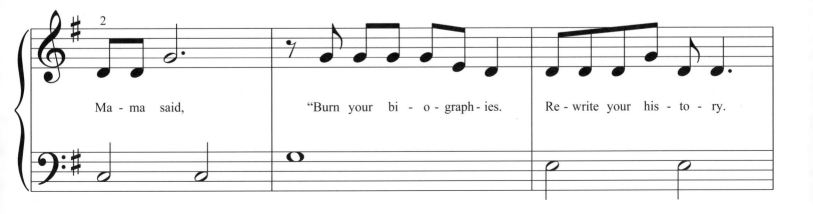

Ma - ma said, "Burn your bi - o - graph - ies. Re - write your his - to - ry.

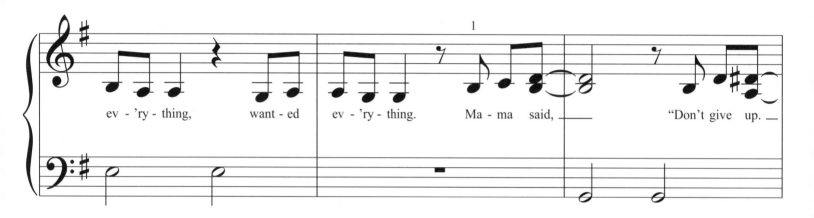

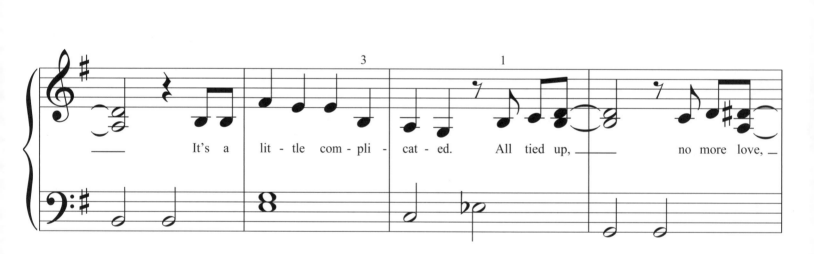

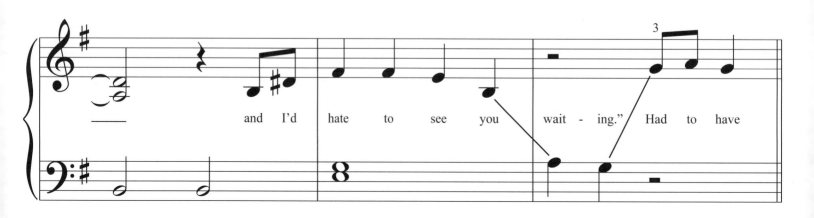

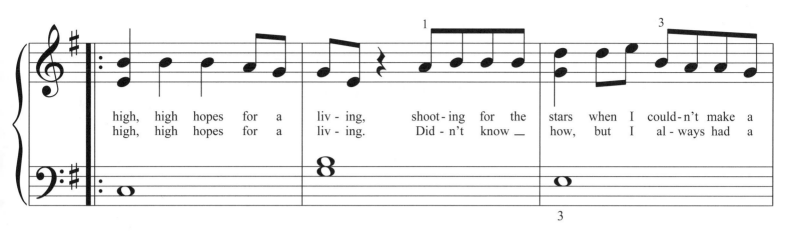

high, high hopes for a liv - ing, shoot - ing for the stars when I could - n't make a
high, high hopes for a liv - ing. Did - n't know __ how, but I al - ways had a

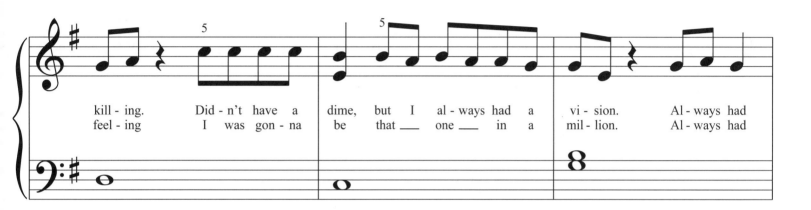

kill - ing. Did - n't have a dime, but I al - ways had a vi - sion. Al - ways had
feel - ing I was gon - na be that __ one __ in a mil - lion. Al - ways had

high, high hopes. __ Had to have
high, high hopes. __ Ma - ma said,

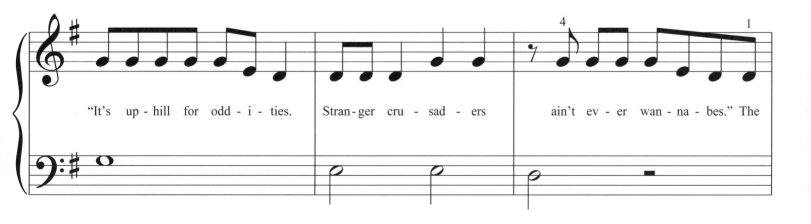

"It's up - hill for odd - i - ties. Stran - ger cru - sad - ers ain't ev - er wan - na - bes." The

weird and the nov - el - ties   don't ev - er   change. ___ We want - ed   ev - 'ry - thing,   want - ed

ev - 'ry - thing.   Stay up on that   rise,   stay up on that

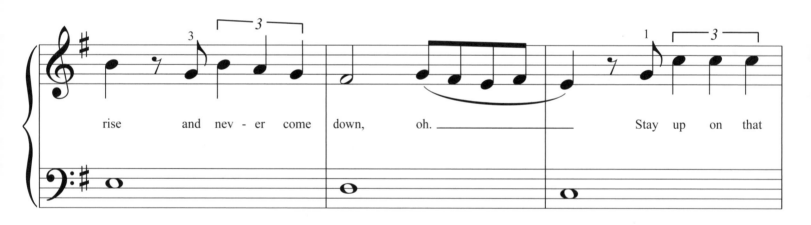

rise   and nev - er come   down,   oh. _____   Stay up on that

rise,   stay up on that   rise   and nev - er come   down.   Ma - ma said, ___

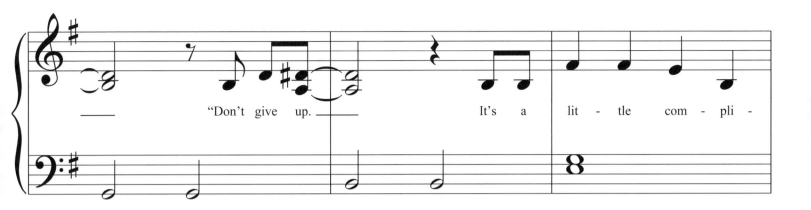

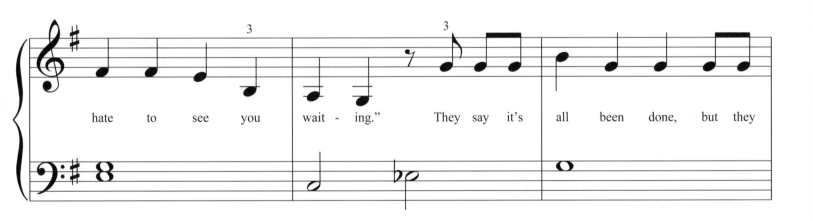

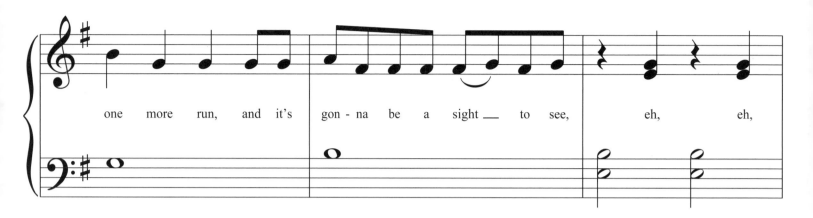

one more run, and it's gon-na be a sight __ to see, eh, eh,

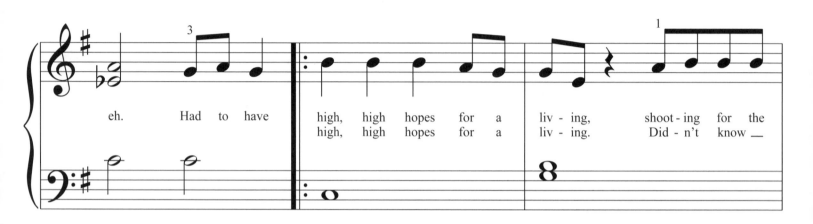

eh. Had to have high, high hopes for a liv-ing, shoot-ing for the
high, high hopes for a liv-ing. Did-n't know __

stars when I could-n't make a kill-ing. Did-n't have a dime, but I al-ways had a
how, but I al-ways had a feel-ing I was gon-na be that __ one __ in a

1.
2.

vi - sion. Al-ways had high, high hopes. __ Had to have
mil-lion. Al-ways had high, high hopes. __

BROKEN

Words and Music by MITCHELL COLLINS,
CHRISTIAN MEDICE and SAMANTHA DeROSA

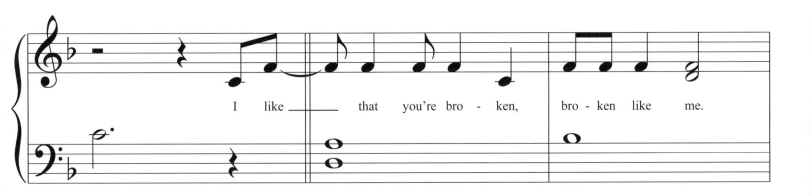

I like ___ that you're bro - ken, bro - ken like me.

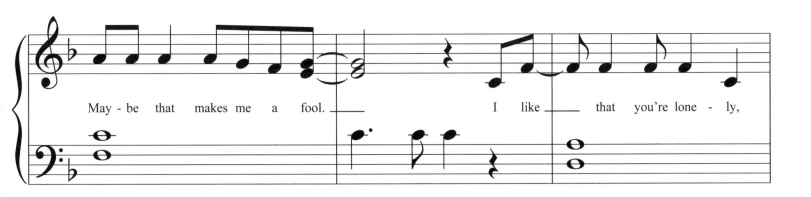

May - be that makes me a fool. ___ I like ___ that you're lone - ly,

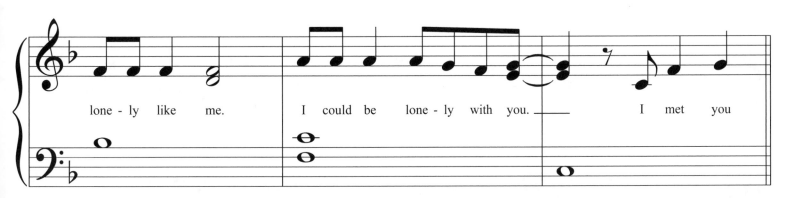

lone - ly like me. I could be lone - ly with you. ___ I met you

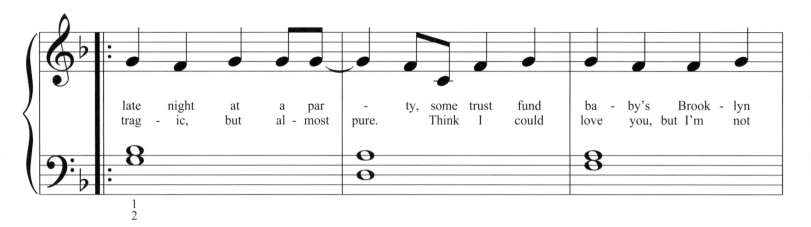

late night at a par - ty, some trust fund ba - by's Brook - lyn

trag - ic, but al - most pure. Think I could love you, but I'm not

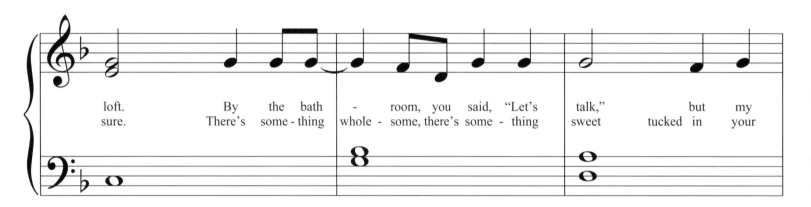

loft. By the bath - room, you said, "Let's talk," but my

sure. There's some - thing whole - some, there's some - thing sweet tucked in your

con - fi - dence was wear - ing off. Well, these aren't my peo - ple, these aren't my

eyes that I'd love to meet.

friends. She grabbed my face and that's when she said: I like that you're bro - ken,

bro-ken like me. May-be that makes me a fool. _____ I like _____ that you're lone - ly,

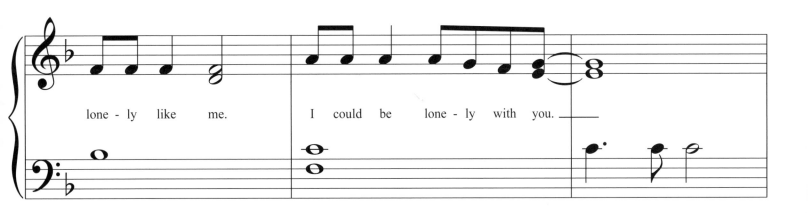

lone - ly like me. I could be lone - ly with you. _____

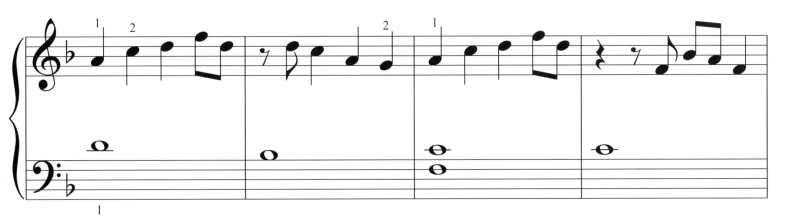

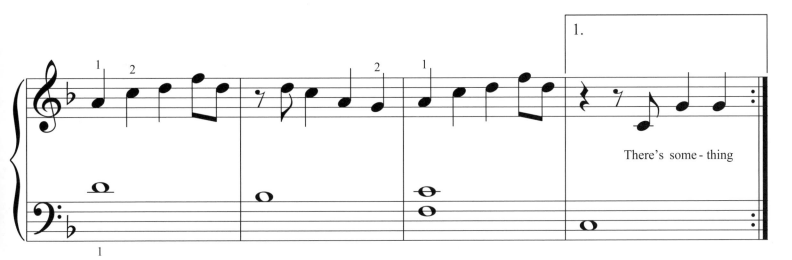

1.

There's some - thing

Well, life is not a love song that we like. We're all bro - ken

piec - es float - ing by. Life is not a love song, we can

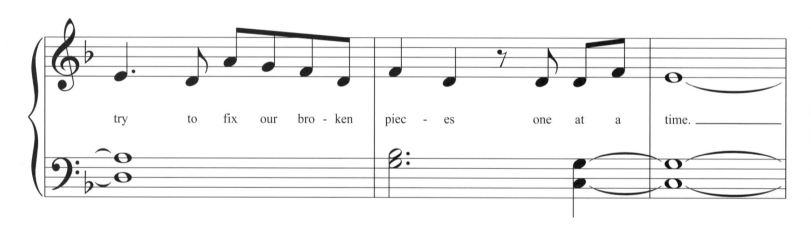

try to fix our bro - ken piec - es one at a time. ____

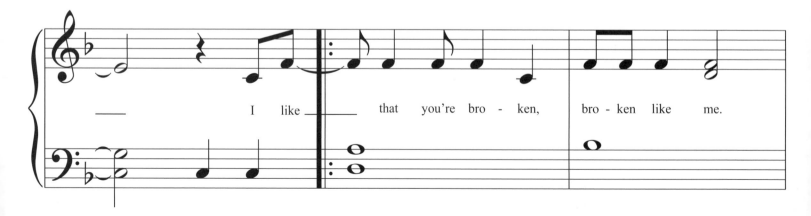

____ I like ____ that you're bro - ken, bro - ken like me.

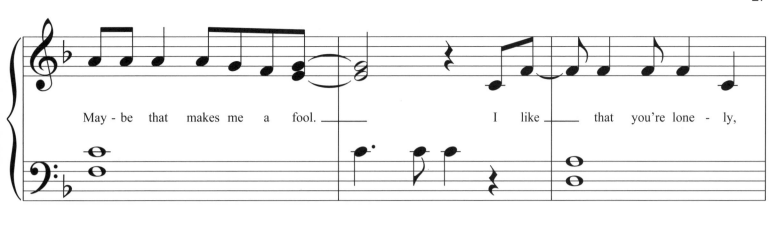

May - be that makes me a fool. I like that you're lone - ly,

lone - ly like me. I could be lone - ly with you. I like

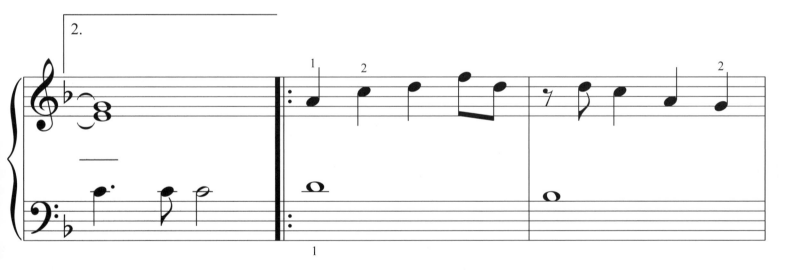

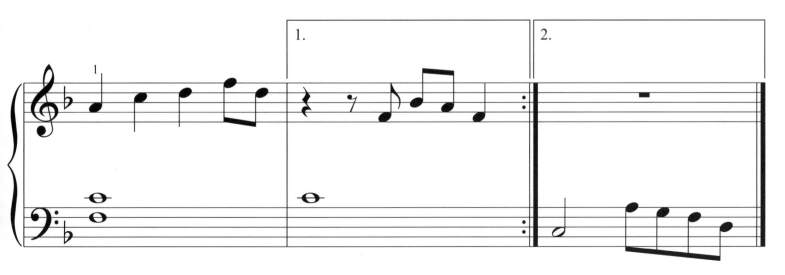

EASTSIDE

Words and Music by BENJAMIN LEVIN,
NATHAN PEREZ, ASHLEY FRANGIPANE,
ED SHEERAN and KHALID ROBINSON

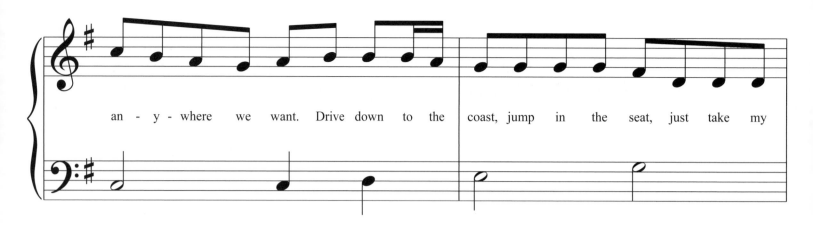

an - y - where we want. Drive down to the coast, jump in the seat, just take my

hand and come with me, yeah. ___ We can do an - y - thing if we put our minds to it.

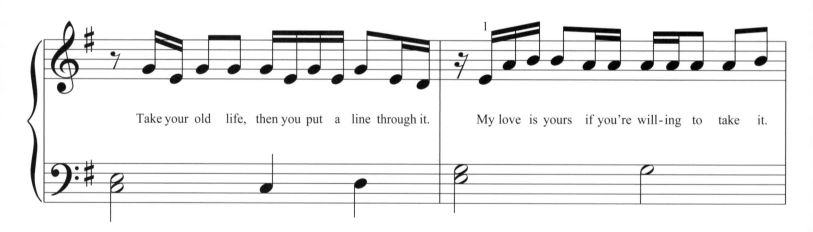

Take your old life, then you put a line through it. My love is yours if you're will - ing to take it.

Give me your heart 'cause I ain't gon - na break it. So, come a - way, start - ing to - day. Start a

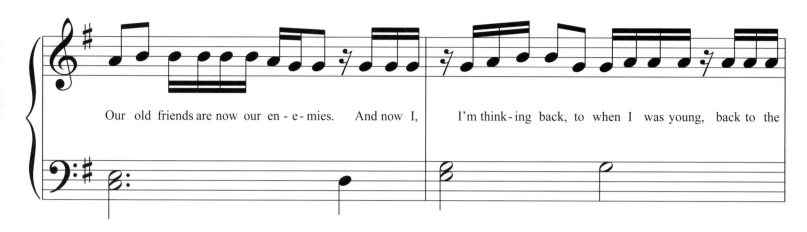

Our old friends are now our en - e - mies. And now I, I'm think - ing back, to when I was young, back to the

D.S. al Coda

day when I was fall - ing in love. He used to meet me on the

CODA

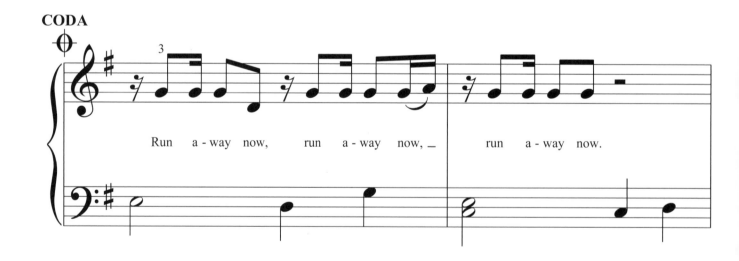

Run a - way now, run a - way now, ___ run a - way now.

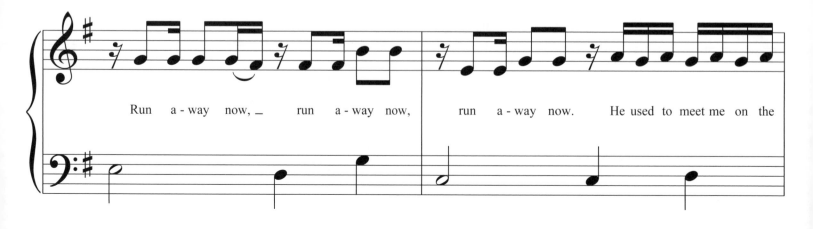

Run a - way now, ___ run a - way now, run a - way now. He used to meet me on the

SHALLOW

from A STAR IS BORN

Words and Music by STEFANI GERMANOTTA,
MARK RONSON, ANDREW WYATT
and ANTHONY ROSSOMANDO

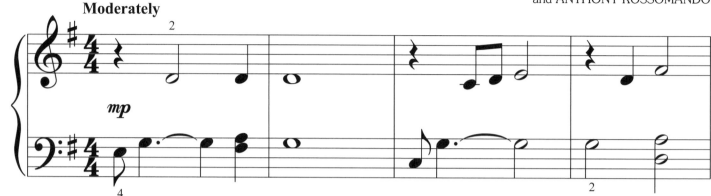

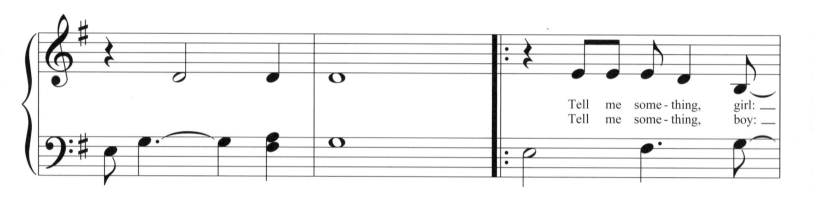

Tell me some-thing, girl:
Tell me some-thing, boy:

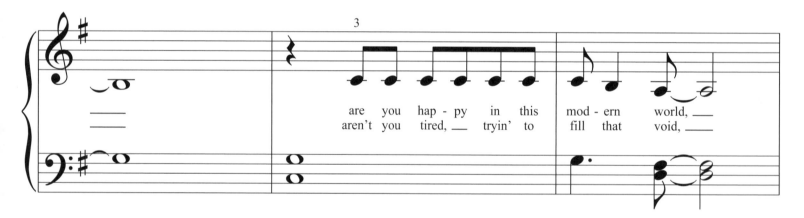

are you hap-py in this mod-ern world, ___
aren't you tired, ___ tryin' to fill that void, ___

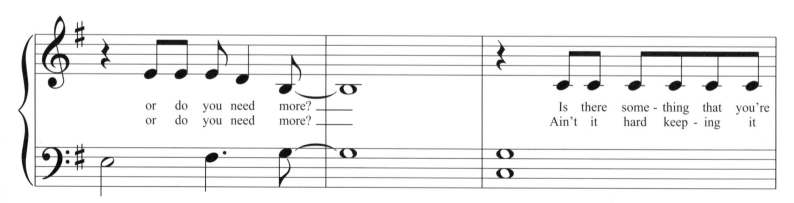

or do you need more? ___
or do you need more? ___

Is there some-thing that you're
Ain't it hard keep-ing it

search - ing   for? ___
so hard - core? ___   I'm   fall -   ing.

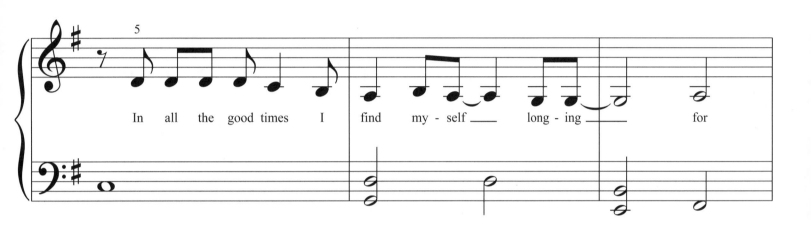

In all the good times I   find my - self ___   long - ing ___   for

change,   and in the bad times I   fear my - self.

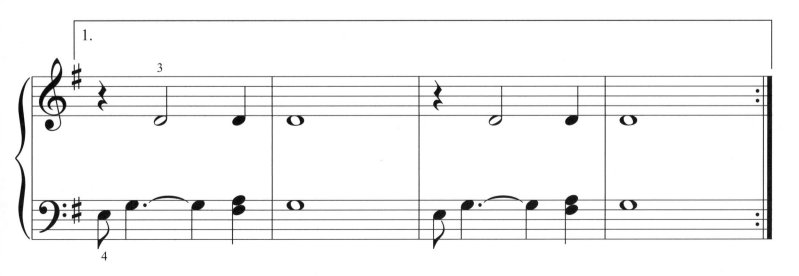

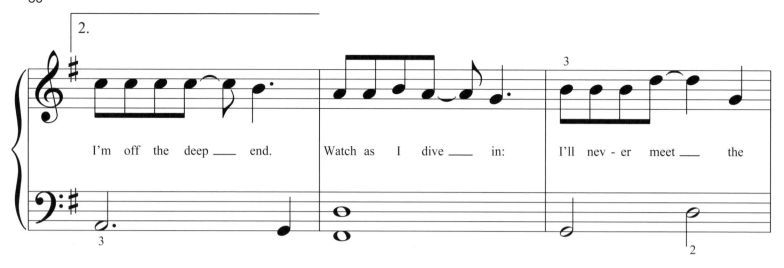

I'm off the deep ___ end.   Watch as I dive ___ in: I'll nev-er meet ___ the

ground. ___   Crash through the sur - face,   where they can't hurt ___ us. We're

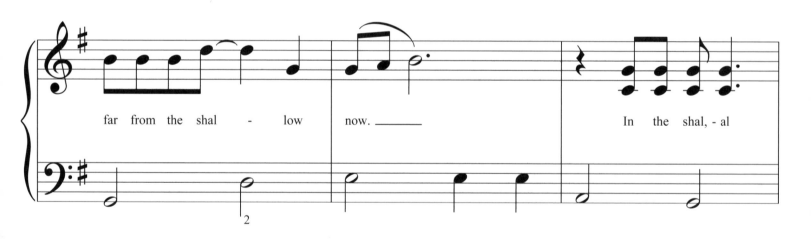

far from the shal - low   now. ___   In the shal, - al

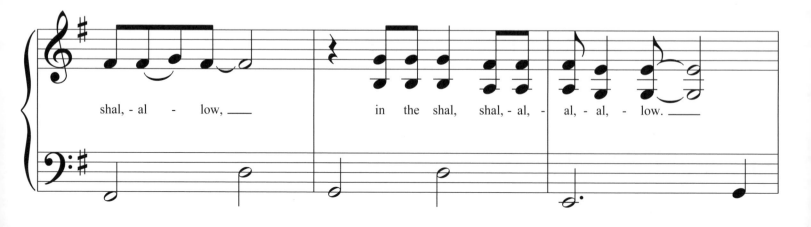

shal, - al - low, ___   in the shal, shal, - al, - al, - al, - low. ___

In the shal, - al, - shal, - al - low, _____ we're far from the shal - low

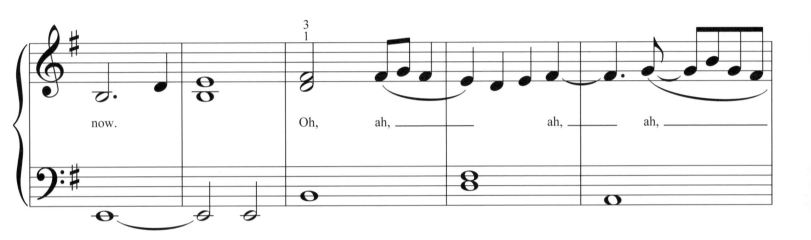

now. Oh, ah, _____ ah, _____ ah, _____

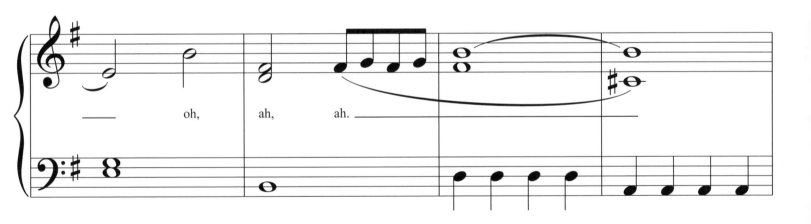

_____ oh, ah, ah. _____

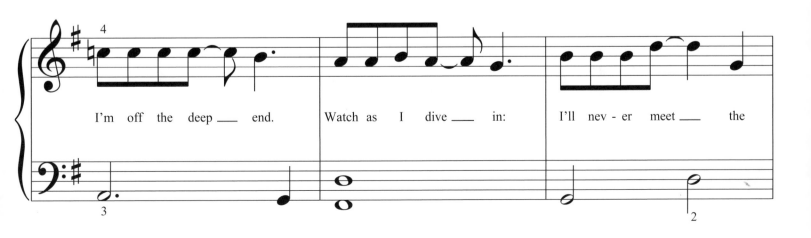

I'm off the deep _____ end. Watch as I dive _____ in: I'll nev - er meet _____ the

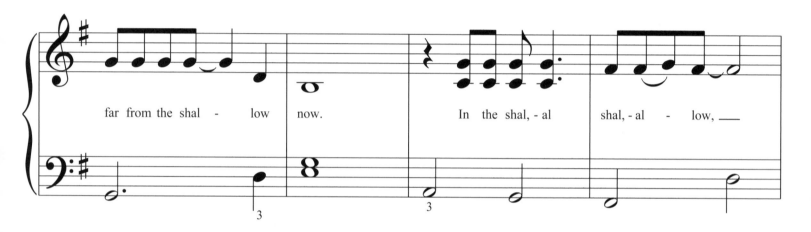

HAPPIER

Words and Music by MARSHMELLO,
STEVE MAC and DAN SMITH

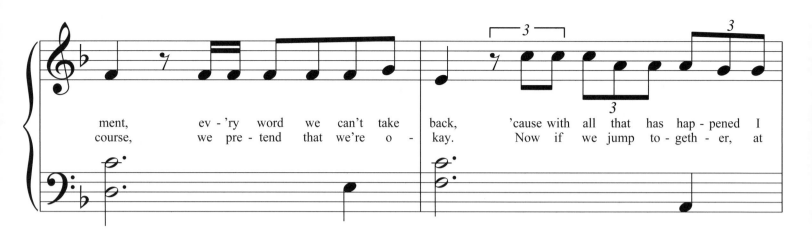

ment, ev - 'ry word we can't take back, 'cause with all that has hap - pened I
course, we pre - tend that we're o - kay. Now if we jump to - geth - er, at

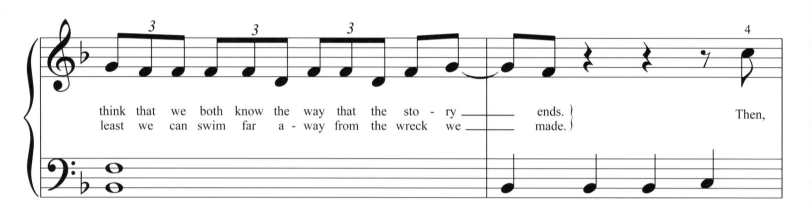

think that we both know the way that the sto - ry ends.
least we can swim far a - way from the wreck we made.   Then,

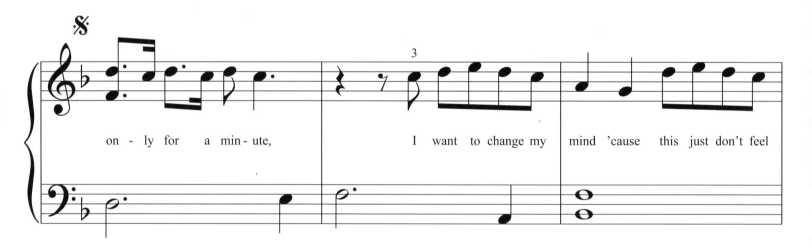

on - ly for a min - ute, I want to change my mind 'cause this just don't feel

right to me. I want to raise your spir - its, I want to see you

smile, but know that means I'll have to leave.

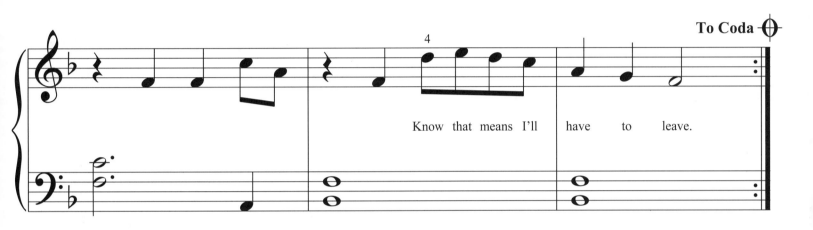

To Coda ⊕

Know that means I'll have to leave.

Late - ly, I've been, I've been think-ing I want you to be hap-pi-er, I want you to be

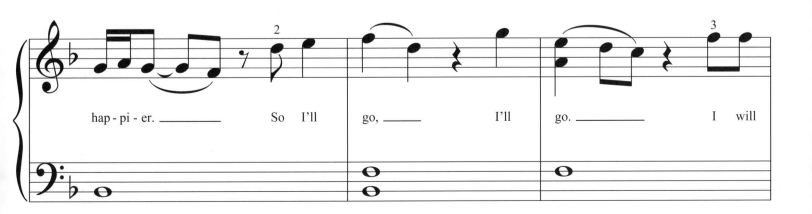

hap-pi-er. _____ So I'll go, _____ I'll go. _____ I will

go,   go,   go.   So I'll   go, _____   I'll   go. _____   I will

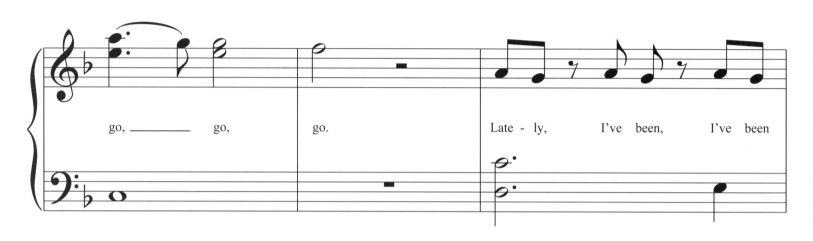

go, _____   go,   go.   Late - ly,   I've been,   I've been

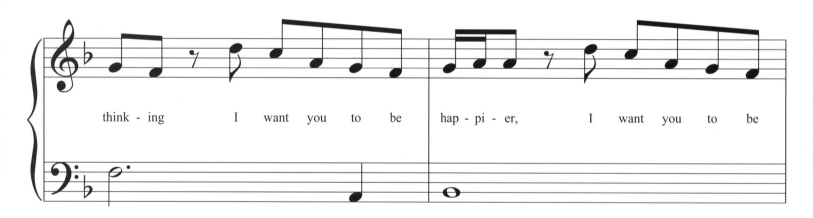

think - ing   I   want you to be   hap - pi - er,   I   want you to be

hap - pi - er.   E - ven   though I   might not   like this,   I think that you'll be

D.S. al Coda
(no repeat)

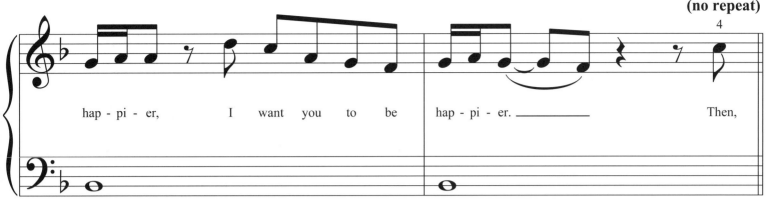

hap - pi - er,   I   want you   to   be   hap - pi - er. _____   Then,

CODA

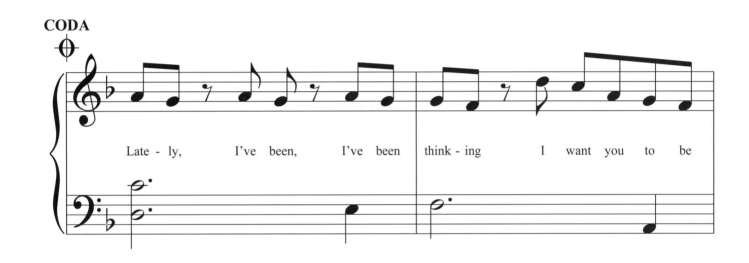

Late - ly,   I've been,   I've been   think - ing   I   want you   to   be

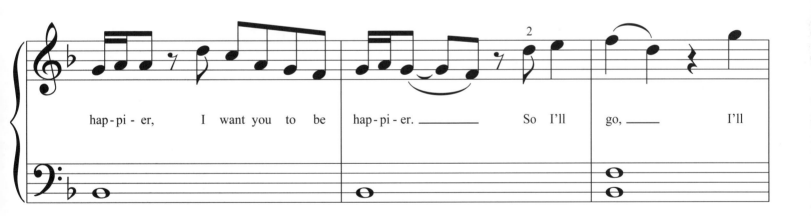

hap - pi - er,   I   want you   to   be   hap - pi - er. _____   So I'll   go, _____   I'll

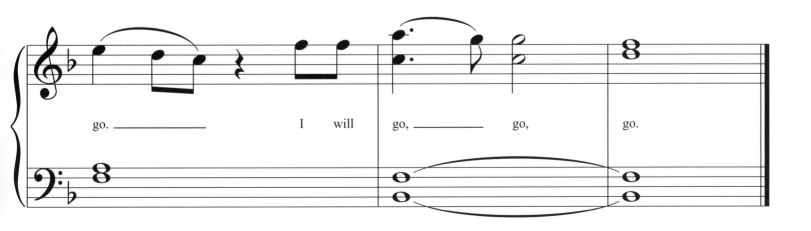

go. _____   I will   go, _____ go,   go.

LOVE SOMEONE

Words and Music by LUKAS FORCHHAMMER,
MORTEN RISTORP, MORTEN PILEGAARD,
JARAMYE DANIELS, DON STEFANO,
DAVID LaBREL and JAMES GHALEB

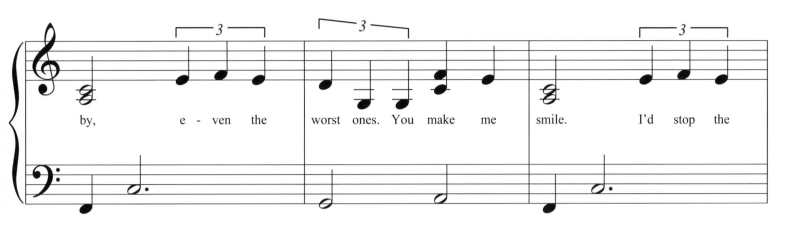

by,　　e - ven the　worst ones. You make me　smile.　　I'd stop the

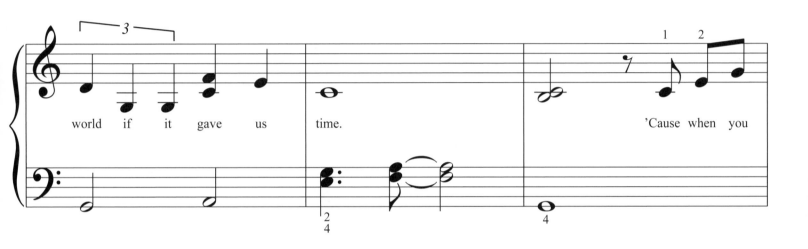

world if　it　gave　us　time.　　　　　　　　　'Cause when you

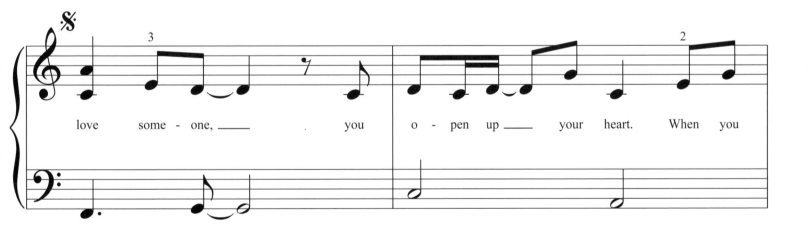

love some - one, ＿＿＿＿　you　o - pen up ＿ your heart. When you

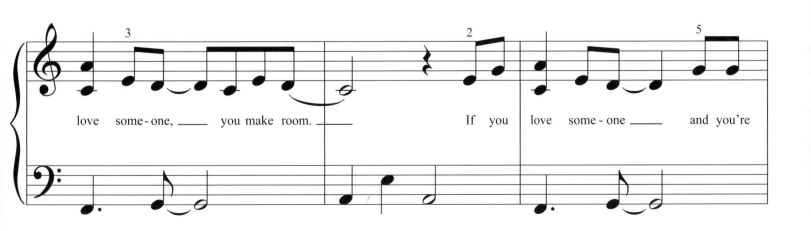

love some - one, ＿ you make room. ＿＿　If　you　love some - one ＿＿ and you're

46

To Coda ⊕

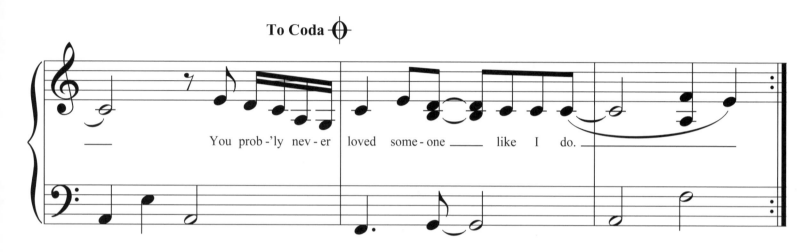

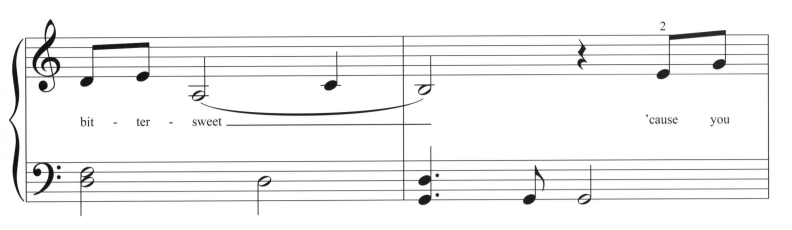

D.S. al Coda

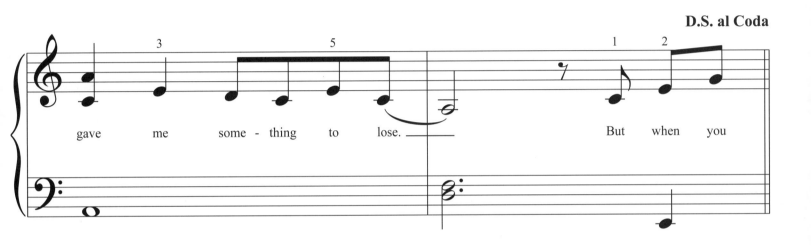

CODA

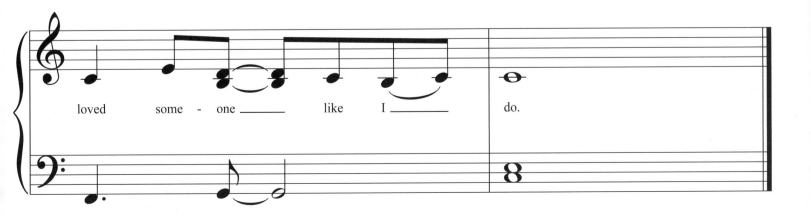

NATURAL

Words and Music by DAN REYNOLDS, WAYNE SERMON,
BEN McKEE, DANIEL PLATZMAN, JUSTIN TRANTOR,
MATTIAS LARSSON and ROBIN FREDRICKSSON

Moderately

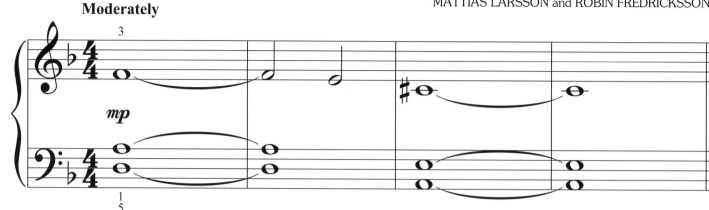

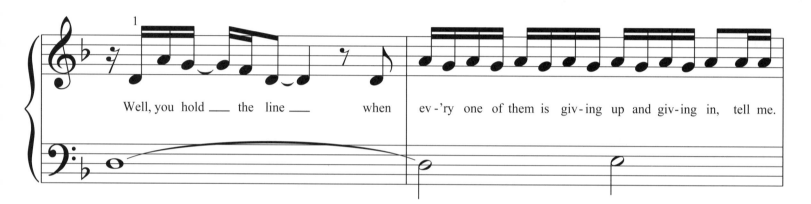

Well, you hold ___ the line ___ when ev-'ry one of them is giv-ing up and giv-ing in, tell me.

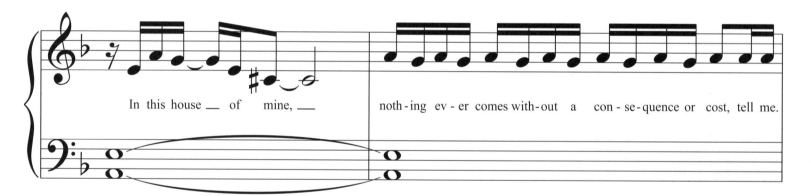

In this house ___ of mine, ___ noth-ing ev-er comes with-out a con-se-quence or cost, tell me.

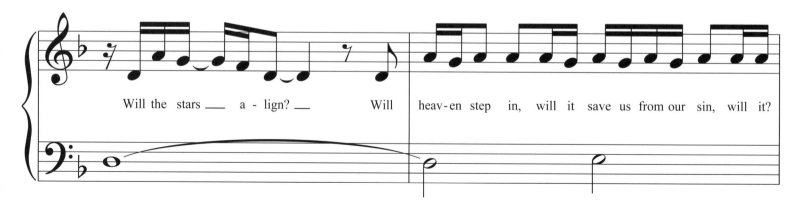

Will the stars ___ a - lign? ___ Will heav-en step in, will it save us from our sin, will it?

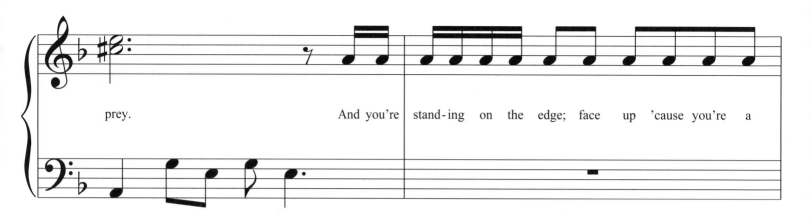

prey.   And you're stand-ing on the edge; face up 'cause you're a

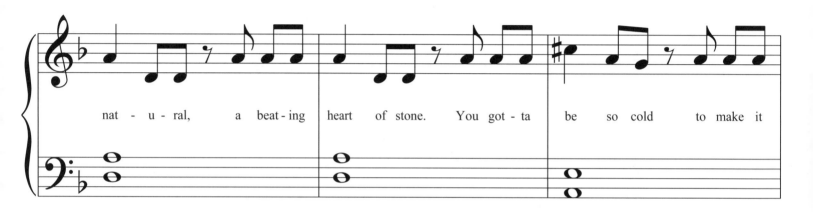

nat - u - ral,   a beat-ing heart of stone. You got-ta be so cold to make it

in this world. Yeah, you're a nat - u - ral, liv-ing your life cut throat. You got-ta

To Coda ⊕

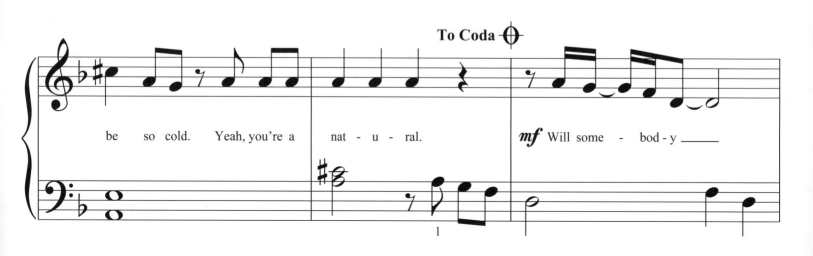

be so cold. Yeah, you're a nat - u - ral.   *mf* Will some - bod - y _____

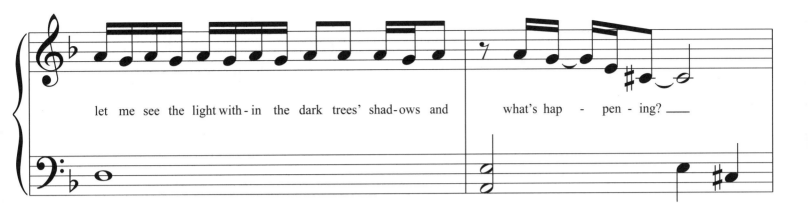

let me see the light with-in the dark trees' shad-ows and what's hap - pen - ing? ____

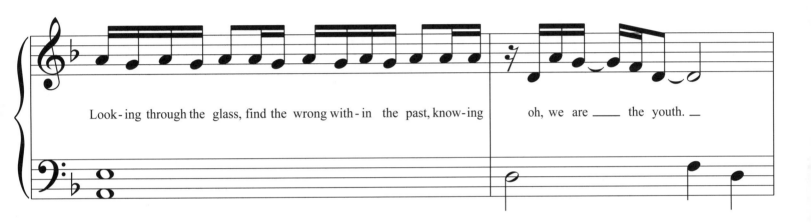

Look-ing through the glass, find the wrong with-in the past, know-ing oh, we are ____ the youth. __

Call out to the beast, not a word with-out the peace, fac-ing a bit of ____ the truth, ____ the truth. __

D.S. al Coda

____ That's the price you pay. ____

CODA

mp Deep in - side me, I'm

fad - ing to black, ___ I'm fad - ing. Took an oath by the

blood of my hand, ___ won't break it. I can taste it; the end is up - on ___ us, I swear.

Gon - na make it, *f* I'm gon - na make it. ___

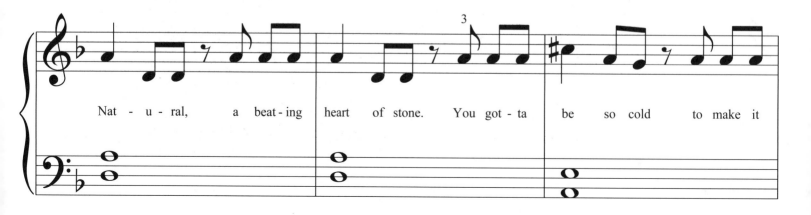

Nat - u - ral, a beat - ing heart of stone. You got - ta be so cold to make it

in this world. Yeah, you're a nat - u - ral, liv - ing your life cut throat. You got - ta

be so cold. Yeah, you're a nat - u - ral.

Nat - u - ral.

Yeah, you're a nat - u - ral.

NOTHING BREAKS LIKE A HEART

Words and Music by MARK RONSON, MILEY CYRUS,
THOMAS BRENNECK, CONOR SZYMANSKI, ILSEY JUBER,
MAXIME MARIE LAURENT PICARD and CLEMENT MARIE JACQUES PICARD

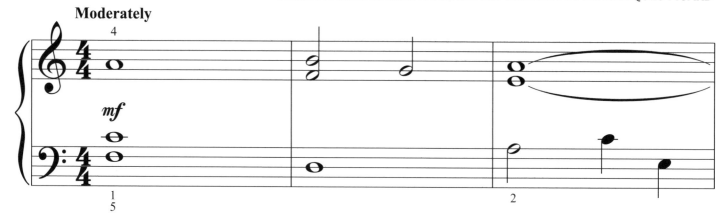

This world can hurt __ you. It cuts you deep and leaves a

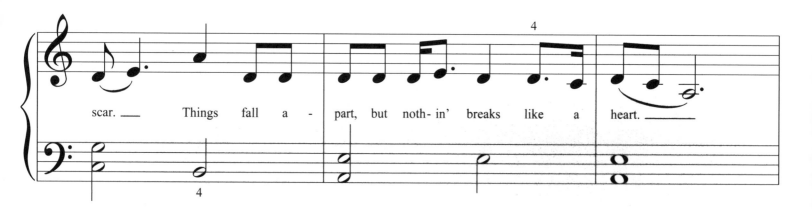

scar. __ Things fall a-part, but noth-in' breaks like a heart. __

Yeah, noth-in' breaks like a heart.   I

heard you on the phone last night. We live and die by pret - ty lies, you

know __ it. We both know __ it. These sil - ver bul - let cig - a - rettes, this

burn - in' house, there's noth - in' left. It's smok - in', we both

know ___ it. We got all night to fall in love, but

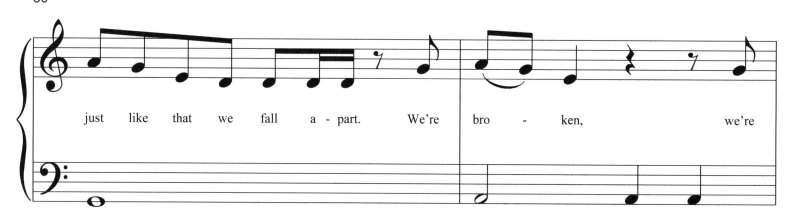

just like that we fall a-part. We're bro - ken, we're

bro - ken. Mmm, well, noth-in', noth-in', noth-in' gon' save us

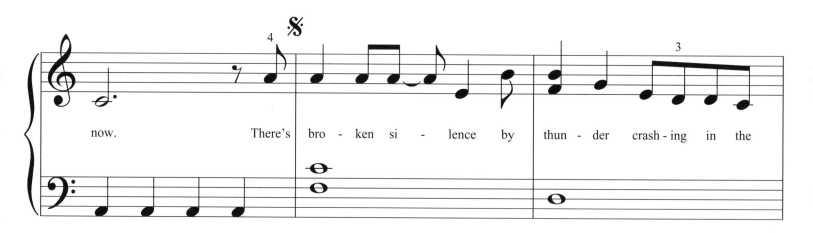

now. There's bro-ken si - lence by thun-der crash-ing in the

dark. (Crash in the dark.) And this bro-ken rec - ord spins

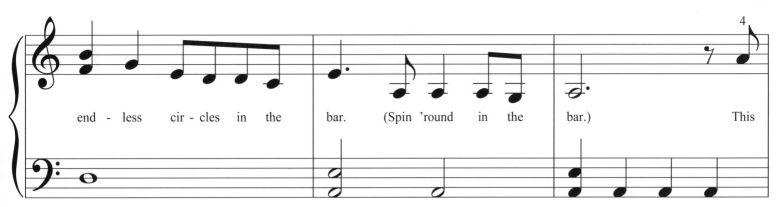

end - less cir - cles in the bar. (Spin 'round in the bar.) This

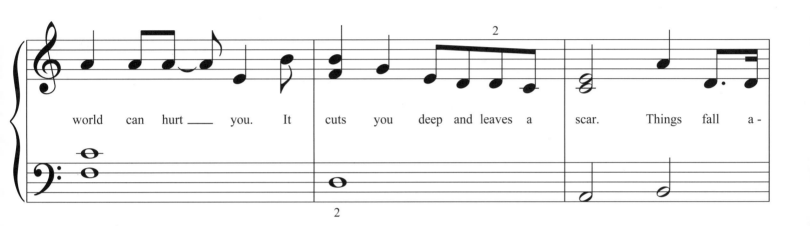

world can hurt ___ you. It cuts you deep and leaves a scar. Things fall a-

part, but noth - in' breaks like a heart. _____ Mm, _____

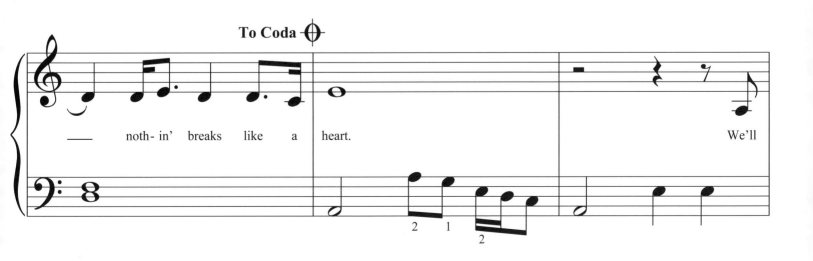

___ noth- in' breaks like a heart. We'll

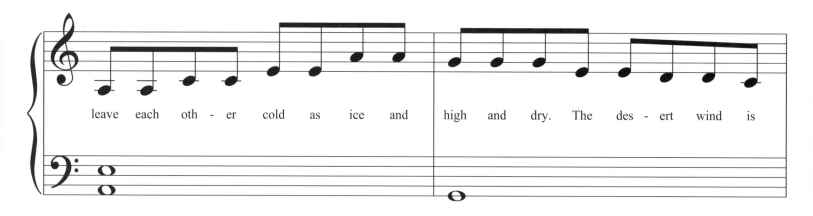

leave each oth - er cold as ice and high and dry. The des - ert wind is

blow - in', is blow - in'. Re - mem - ber what you said to me? We were

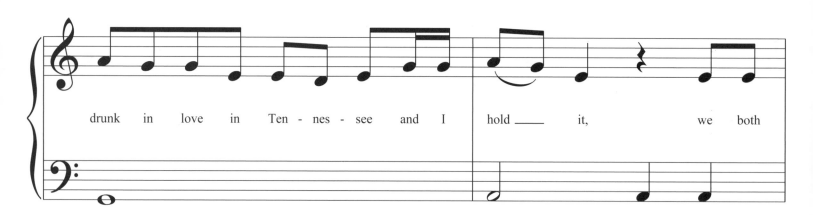

drunk in love in Ten - nes - see and I hold _____ it, we both

know _____ it. Mmm, there's noth - in', noth - in', noth - in' gon' save us

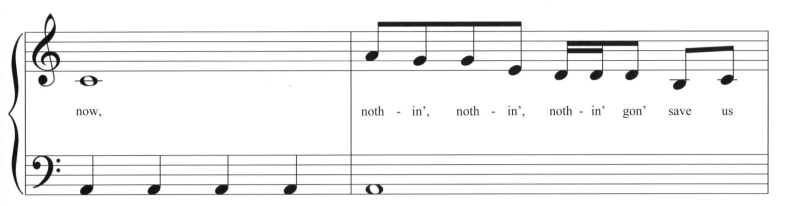

now, noth - in', noth - in', noth - in' gon' save us

D.S. al Coda **CODA**

now. There's heart. Noth- in' breaks like a

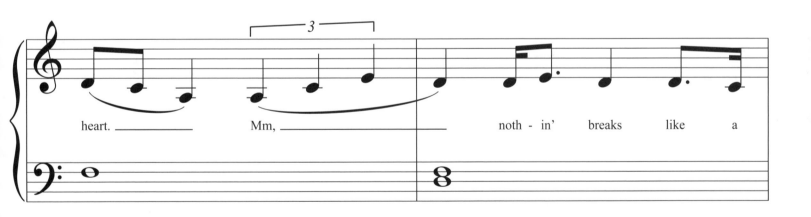

heart. _____ Mm, _____ noth - in' breaks like a

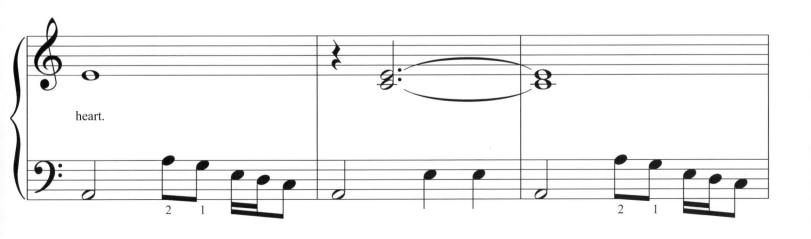

heart.

And noth-in', noth-in', noth-in' gon' save us now,

noth-in', noth-in', noth-in' gon' save us now. There's bro-ken si - lence by

thun - der crash - ing in the dark. (Crash in the dark.) And this

bro - ken rec - ord spins end - less cir - cles in the bar. (Spin 'round in the

bar.) This world can hurt ___ you. It cuts you deep and leaves a

scar. Things fall a - part, but noth - in' breaks like a heart. ___ Mm, ___

___ noth - in' breaks like a heart. Noth - in' breaks like a

heart. ___ Mm, ___ noth - in' breaks like a heart.

SUNFLOWER
from SPIDER-MAN: INTO THE SPIDER-VERSE

Words and Music by AUSTIN RICHARD POST,
LOUIS BELL, SWAE LEE, BILLY WALSH,
CARL ROSEN, CARTER LANG and KHALIF BROWN

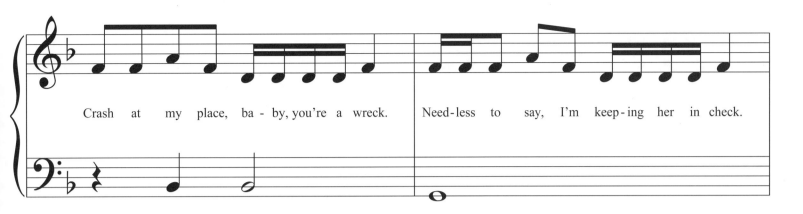

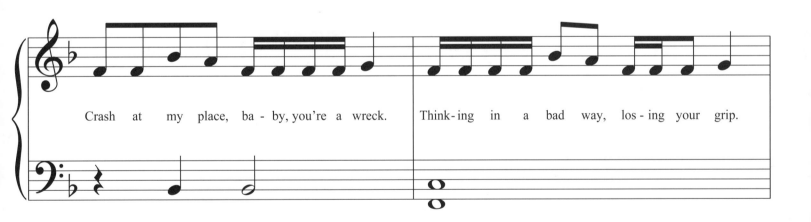

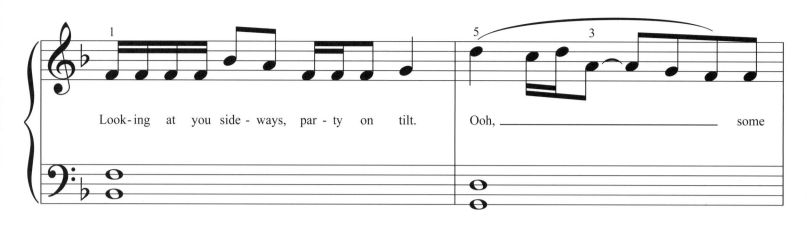

Look-ing at you side-ways, par-ty on tilt. Ooh, _____ some

things you just can't re-fuse. _____ She wan-na ride like a cruise, _____ and I'm

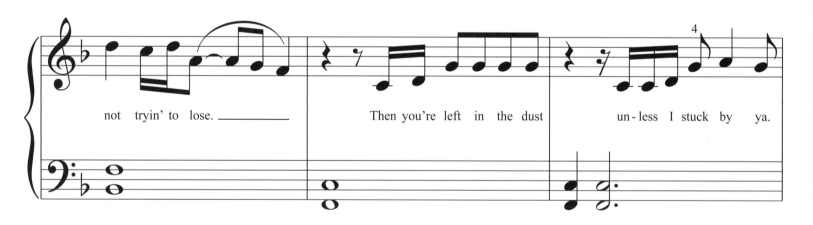

not tryin' to lose. _____ Then you're left in the dust un-less I stuck by ya.

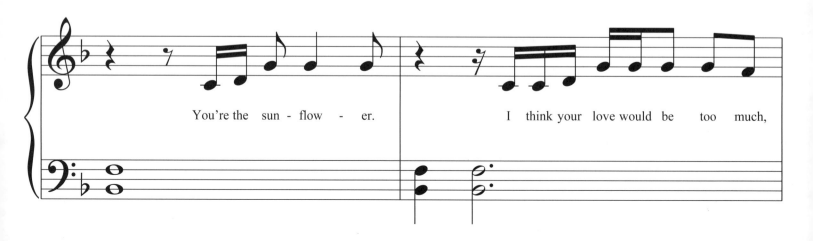

You're the sun-flow-er. I think your love would be too much,

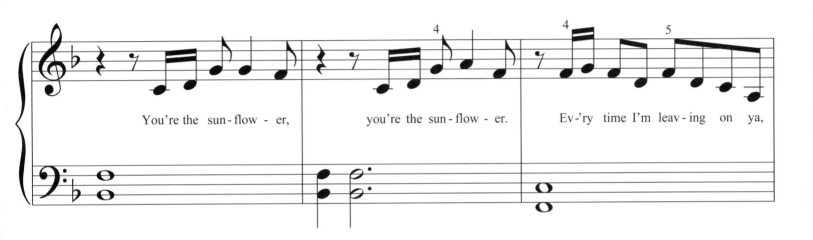

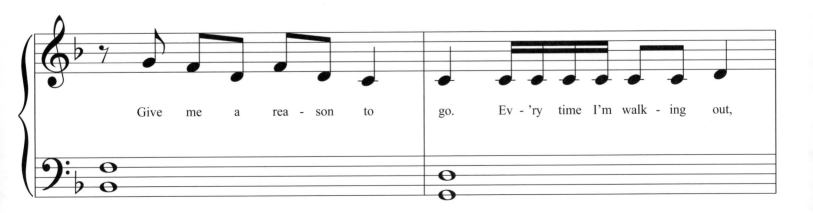

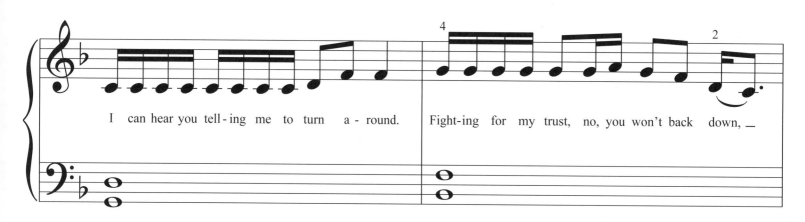

I can hear you tell-ing me to turn a-round.

Fight-ing for my trust, no, you won't back down, ___

e-ven if we got-ta risk it all right now. ___

I know you're scared of the un-known, ___

you don't wan-na be a-lone. ___

I know I al-ways come and go, ___

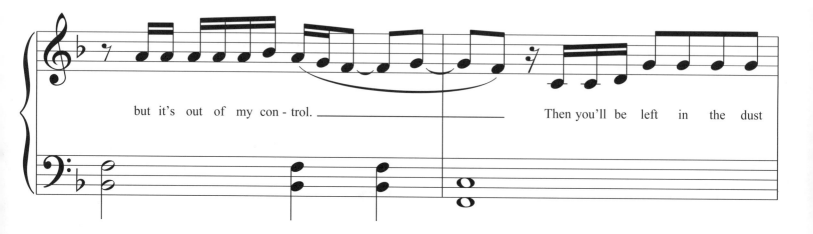

but it's out of my con-trol. ___

Then you'll be left in the dust

un - less I stuck by ya.   You're the sun - flow - er.

I think your love would be   too much,   or you'll be left in the dust

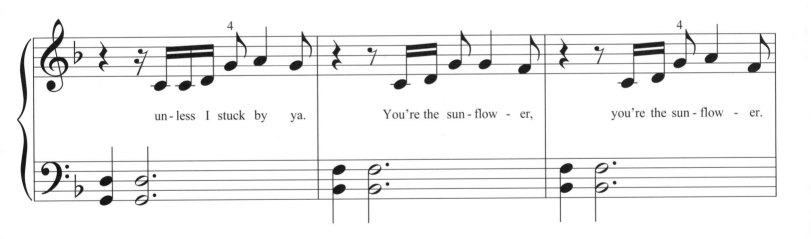

un - less I stuck by ya.   You're the sun - flow - er,   you're the sun - flow - er.

TRIP

Words and Music by ELLA MAI HOWELL, DIJON McFARLANE,
VARREN JEROME LLOYD WADE and QUINTON COOK

Moderately slow

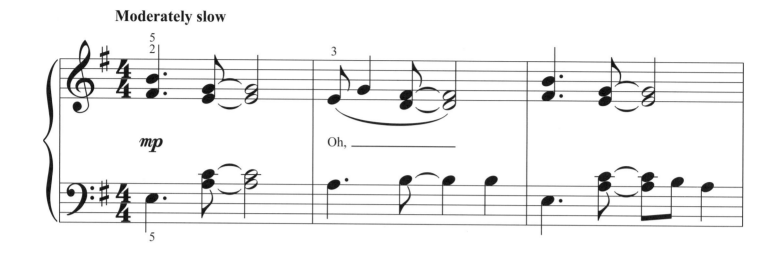

I put my feel-ings on safe-ty_____ so I don't go
cool now you're wait-in', _____ but I act a

shoot-ing where your heart __ be. _____ 'Cause you take the
fool when I don't get __ it. _____ And I'm stead-y

bul-let try-na save me. _____ Then I'm left to
bruis-in' just to save this, _____ I tripped on your

deal with mak-in' you __bleed.
love, now I'm ad-dict - ed.
And that's a whole lot-ta love, __ain't try-na waste it. Like we be run-nin' a mile __

__ and nev-er make it. That's just too bit-ter for words, __don't wan-na taste it. That's just too bit-ter for words, __

__ don't wan-na face it. __ But I think that I'm done trip-pin', I'm trip, trip-pin',

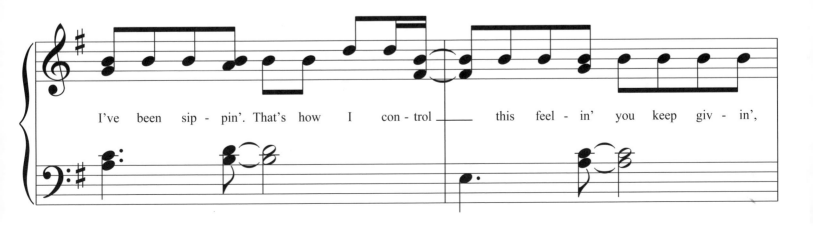

I've been sip-pin'. That's how I con-trol __ this feel-in' you keep giv-in',

you keep on hit-tin' it, ooh, oh. May-be it's your love, it's too good to be true. Ba-by boy, your

love got me trip-pin' on you. You know your love is big e-nough, make me trip up on ya. Yeah, it's big e-

nough, got me trip-pin' on ya, trip, trip-pin' on ya. My bad, my bad for trip-pin' on you.

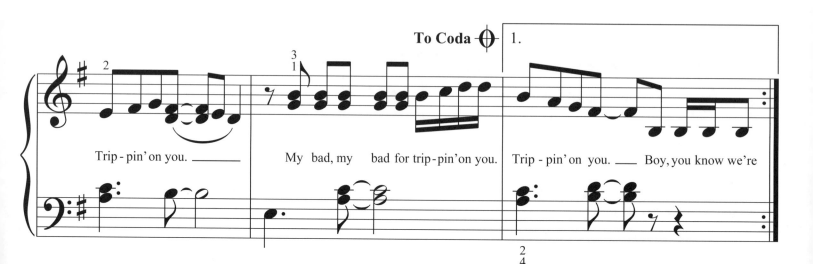

Trip-pin' on you. _____ My bad, my bad for trip-pin' on you. Trip-pin' on you. _____ Boy, you know we're

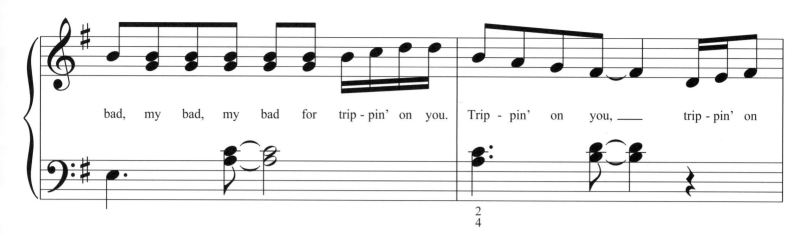

bad, my bad, my bad for trip-pin' on you. Trip-pin' on you, ___ trip-pin' on

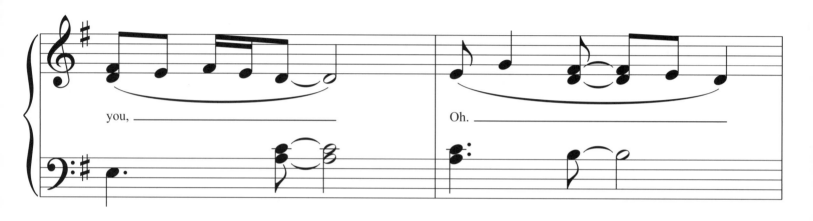

you, ___ Oh. ___

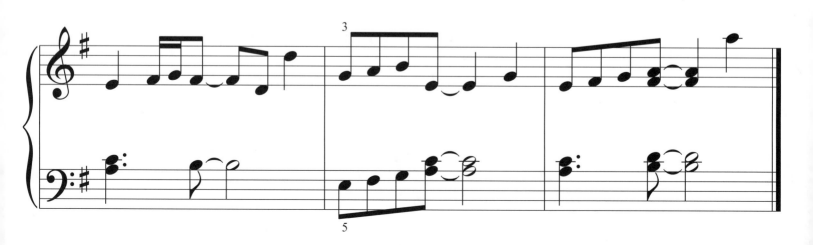

YOUNGBLOOD

Words and Music by ASHTON IRWIN,
CALUM HOOD, LOUIS BELL, LUKE HEMMING,
ALEXANDRA TAMPOSI and ANDREW WATT

Moderately fast

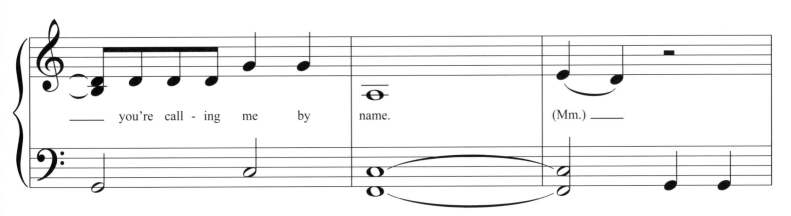

74

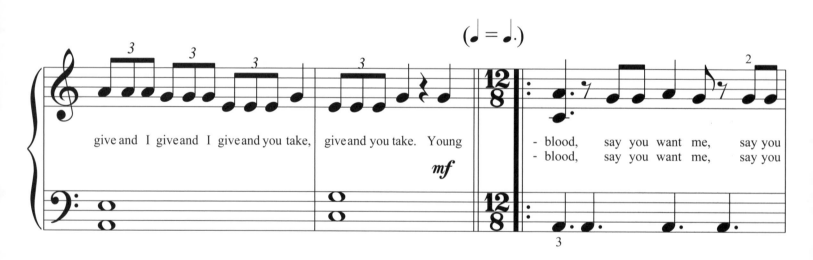

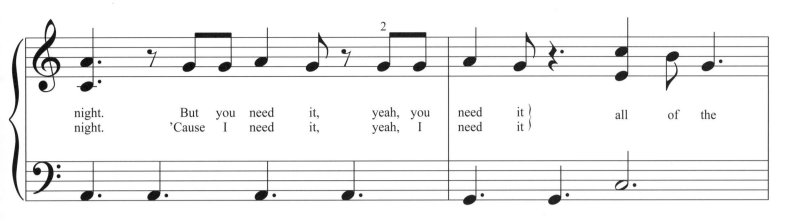

night.   But you need it,   yeah, you   need it   all of the
night.   'Cause I need it,   yeah, I   need it

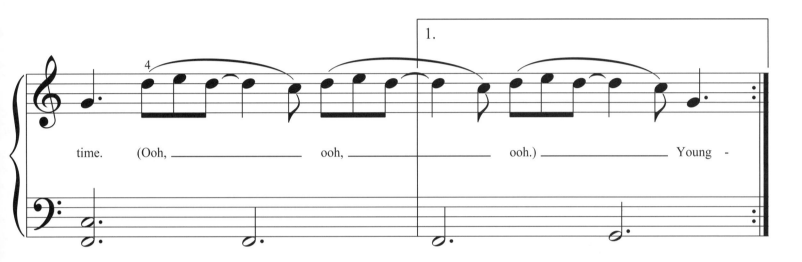

time. (Ooh, _____ ooh, _____ ooh.) _____ Young -

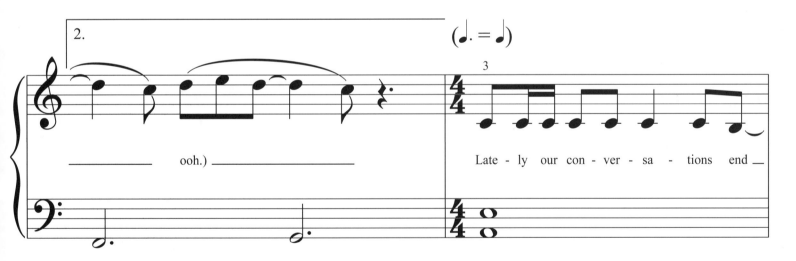

_____ ooh.) _____   Late - ly our con - ver - sa - tions end

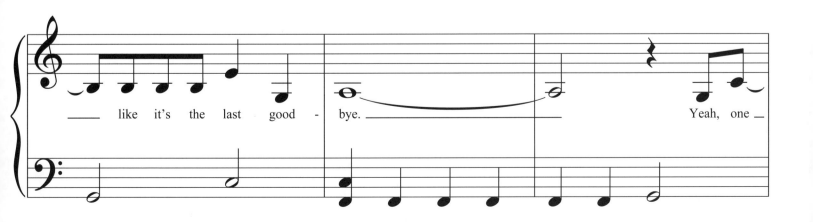

____ like it's the last good - bye. _____   Yeah, one __

of us gets too drunk and calls a - bout a hun - dred times.

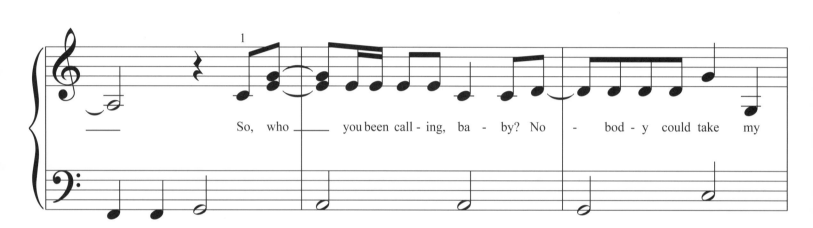

So, who you been call - ing, ba - by? No - bod - y could take my

place. When you're look - ing at those stran - gers, hope

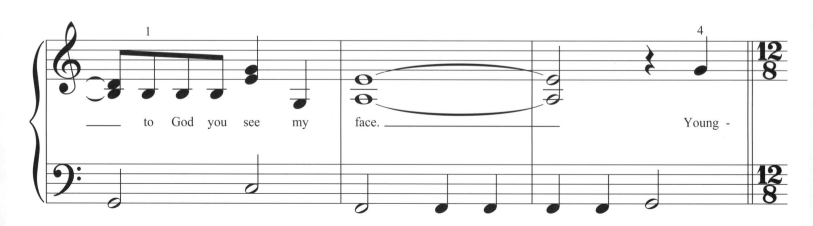

to God you see my face. Young -

give and I give and I give and you take, give and you take. I'm run-ning a-round and I'm run-ning a-way,

run-ning a-way from you, mm, from you. Young -

blood, say you want me, say you want me out of your life, and I'm just a
blood, say you want me, say you want me back in your life, so I'm just a

dead man walk-ing to - night. But you need it, yeah, you need it } all of the
dead man crawl-ing to - night. 'Cause I need it, yeah, I need it } all of the

WITHOUT ME

Words and Music by ASHLEY FRANGIPANE, BRITTANY AMARADIO,
CARL ROSEN, JUSTIN TIMBERLAKE, SCOTT STORCH,
LOUIS BELL, AMY ALLEN and TIMOTHY MOSLEY

Slow R&B groove

Found you when your heart was broke. I filled your cup un-til it o-ver-flowed. Took it
Gave love 'bout a hun-dred tries. Just run-ning from the de-mons in your mind. Then I

so far to keep you close. I was a-fraid to leave you on your own. I said I'd
took yours and made them mine. I did-n't no-tice 'cause my love was blind.

catch you if you fall, ____ and if they laugh, then leave 'em all. ____ And then I

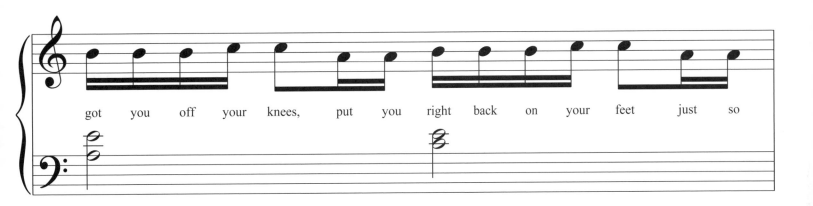

got you off your knees, put you right back on your feet just so

you could take ad - van - tage of me. Tell me: how's it feel ____ sit - ting up there, feel - ing so

high, but too far a - way to hold me? You know I'm the one who put you up there, name in the

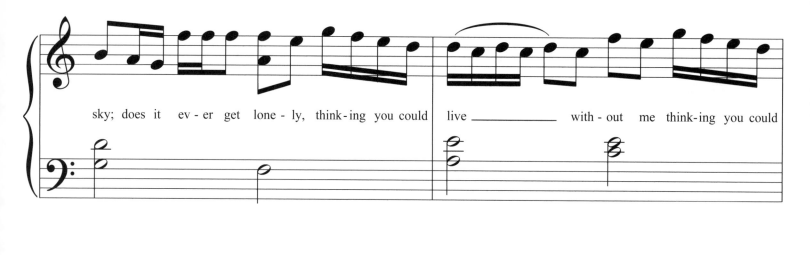

sky; does it ev - er get lone - ly, think-ing you could live _____ with - out me think-ing you could

To Coda ⊕

live _____ with - out me? Ba - by, I'm the one who put you up there. I don't know

why. (Don't know why.) Think-ing you could live _____ with - out me,

live _____ with - out me? Ba - by, I'm the one who put you up there. I don't know

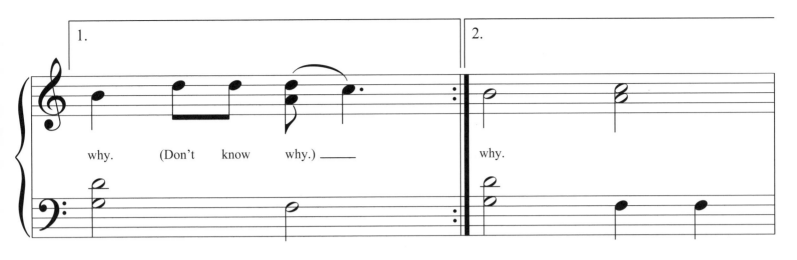

1.

why. (Don't know why.) _____

2.

why.

You don't have to say just what you did; I know. _____ I had to go and find out from

D.S. al Coda

them. So tell me: how's it feel? _____ Tell me: how's it

CODA

why. (Don't know why.)

YOU SAY

Words and Music by LAUREN DAIGLE,
JASON INGRAM and PAUL MABURY

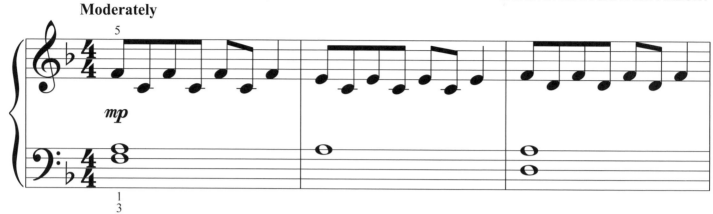

I keep fight-ing voic-es in my mind that say I'm not e-nough,

ev-'ry sin-gle lie that tells me

I will nev-er meas-ure up.

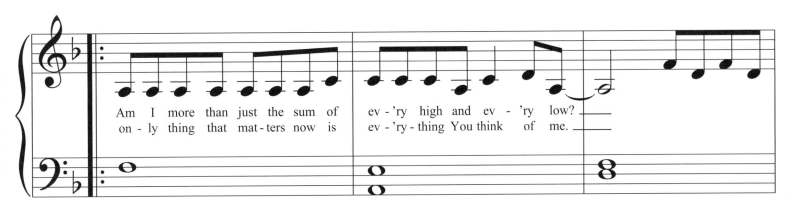

85

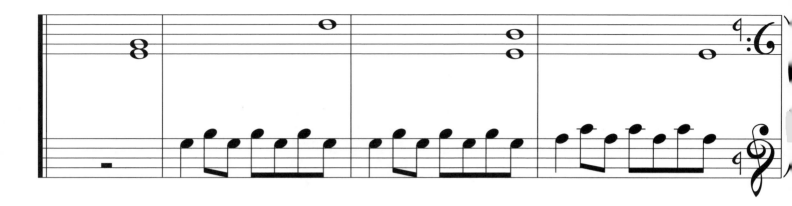
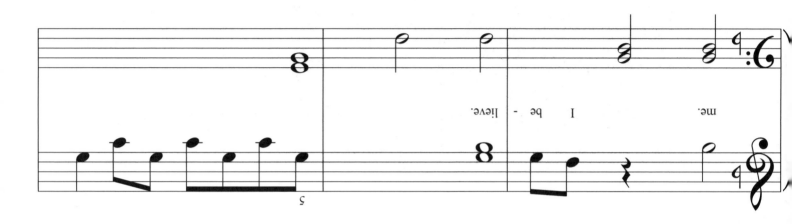
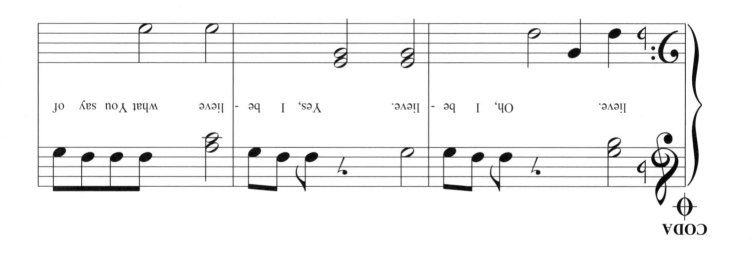
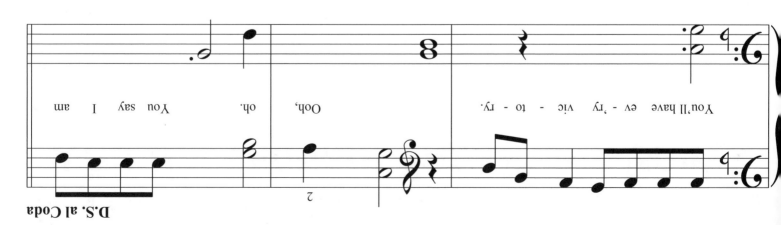

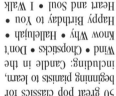

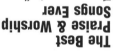